First published in Great Britain, 2008, as
The Weeping Redwood Tree
by Church Path Publishing

Copyright © Kevin Scott 2002

The moral right of the author of this work has been asserted.

Cover Photograph by Kevin Scott

Church Path Publishing
Church Cottage, Church Path, Rotherfield
East Sussex, TN6 3FD, UK
Email: churchpathpublishing@hotmail.co.uk

Lost Soul Saved

Written in response to an ecclesiastical historian who maintained that 'nobody was entitled to forgiveness.' It was not clear if the gentleman included himself.

Lost Soul Saved

In the great redwood forest, a gentle breeze softly sighed through tree branches high above the ground. A lone elderly gentleman knelt silently at the base of a giant sequoia. Small birds and animals had grown accustomed to his presence. They did not notice the rise and fall of his shoulders or the flow of tears that streaked his hollow cheeks. They were not aware of the length of the man's years or the questions that tormented his mind and heart. The stillness was broken when the man shouted.

"God! Why am I lost? What happened to the young man who was comforted by your healing touch and ordained to serve you? Where is the pleasure I felt from every divine thought? Why is secularism threatening the Church? Dear God, why are you deserting me?"

His voice reached fever pitch, breaking with emotion. Animals rushed into hiding from a fury they did not comprehend. The forest fell silent again. He waited for a response on the echo of his plea but there was no echo, no response. His cry was lost in thick growth that absorbed all sound. The man sighed and covered his eyes, not wanting to see the majestic beauty that replied not to his entreaties. At hearing a distant rumble he uncovered his eyes and looked in the direction of the sound.

The forest was filled with a surging roar as a powerful wind swept through the trees. He covered his ears but the wind was about to sweep him off his feet. He turned and clung to strips of bark as the gale lashed him with brush and duff. Long, bony fingers dug deeper into the thick bark as the storm attempted to wrench him from the tree. The storm faded as fast as it began. Peace returned.

The old gentleman loosened his grip and lightly rested his head against the soft, spongy bark. He whispered, "Why do you not answer me?"

Why do you not listen?

The man staggered backwards, stumbled into a cushion of redwood needles and ferns. He swept aside a piece of fern from his face, struggled to his feet, brushed debris from his clothing and gazed in astonishment at the giant sequoia. "You certainly took me by surprise."

Obviously!

"Well." He said confidently. "Now that you finally hear my voice, perhaps you will be kind enough to answer my questions."

I heard your voice from the beginning. You did not hear my responses because you were not listening.

"I do not accept that. I prayed constantly, century after century. Only now do I hear your voice."

You were listening to your own voice, which was

given you by those you believed were teaching in my name.

"That is not true! I faithfully followed traditions and teachings of all souls in whom Christ has been welcomed."

Are you confused?

"I certainly am not!"

You just confirmed that you followed those you believed were teaching in my name, then admitted this is the first time you hear my voice. They are not the same. Your traditions are irrevocably linked to the manifestations of men. You, in common with most of your species, cling to traditions as if they are solid unchanging foundations of all that is holy.

The old man frowned. Deep in thought he slowly circled the tree, returned to where he began, stopped and scratched his head. "Surely you are not suggesting that I have not been faithful to truth?"

That is precisely my meaning. My truth is eternal. Traditions are brief reflections of human history.

"How dare you make such a preposterous suggestion? I have kept the faith. We are dependent on our knowledge and teachings of Christ on a continuous line of believers. I have been the body of the Lord in the world for nearly two thousand years!" He jabbed a gnarled finger into the bark. "That is probably as long as you have been rooted where you now stand!"

This tree has been here a mere fifteen hundred years. I created the universe more than fifteen thousand million years ago. As of this moment you no longer need to rely on faith.

For a second time the elderly man staggered backwards, just managing to stay upright. He roared with laughter. "And who do you think you are – God?"

That is a name by which you claim to know me.

"Oh, dear," he mumbled as he prostrated himself before the giant redwood tree. "I thought I was talking to the tree."

I am everywhere and in everything.

"Are you actually speaking to this miserable wretch filled with doubt and plagued by questions that lavish great weight on my suffering?"

Your heartfelt pleas removed an obstacle and opened your soul. Are you now willing to open your mind?

"Oh, yes!"

It may be difficult since you place great importance on tradition and sincere instruction from respected scholars.

"Are you implying that scholarship is of little value?"

It is extremely valuable to those seeking knowledge of the world. Do not underestimate the importance of scholarship. Neither should you undervalue intuitive knowledge that resides within every person's innermost being. Scholarship is learned. Knowledge of divine essence cannot be acquired intellectually.

The old man swallowed his pride and slowly sat facing the tree. "I am ready." An audible sigh was heard, as if nature itself was relieved by the unfolding scene. A northern spotted owl, eyeing a vole, was distracted by the dialogue that was captivating the forest. The owl, not wanting to miss a single word, lunged from its high platform, swooped close to the man's head and landed nearby.

Long before you came into existence there was great turmoil among your species over whom correctly understood and interpreted my nature and thought. As you know, there were terrible wars and much shedding of blood as one belief attempted to crush so-called nonbelievers, those who disputed particular assumptions. It apparently escaped the attention of religious leaders that great spiritual revelation is rooted in genuine understanding of the essence of creation. Comprehension does not always mirror the excellence of true revelation.

Divisions developed through misunderstanding; a danger inherent in evolution as life forms mutate to survive changing environments. In common with many beliefs you were, at some point, isolated from spiritual understanding and became entrenched in traditional interpretations of truth. For example you admitted faithfully following the teachings of souls in whom Christ had been welcomed, but ignore the possibility that interpretations and translations might have been flawed. You pray I will lead you not into temptation; as if I would. The old Palestinian Hebrew dialect spoken by Jesus was misinterpreted by Greeks. My son prayed, 'Let us not enter temptation'.

You sincerely believe you remained obedient to my word. Institutionalized customs became the focus – the seat of men's individual and collective acceptance. They are followed by sheep who feel secure in large herds, too lazy to search for the truth that resides within, waiting to be heard. Do you understand?

The ancient man thought carefully before answering. "Not entirely. The foundation of our teaching has always been firmly established on your undeserved love, the salvation of the world through your grace and the sacrifice on the cross of your son, Christ Jesus."

You speak well. You worship Jesus as my only son. In so doing you failed to recognize countless sons and daughters who were sent to aid under-

8

standing of the purpose of creation. You alienated those who recognized other sons and daughters sent to help them. My children conveyed messages in languages and symbols most easily understood by disparate cultures. Instead of recognizing the similarity of teaching in the context of differing cultures you purged and murdered and persecuted. You were not alone, and are still not alone in this terrible injustice.

Powerful nations are hated by those who feel threatened by might. Mighty nations grow in stature when they respond compassionately to hatred whenever possible. Men commit atrocities against themselves and others in my name. Although recognized in every heart, it is not readily admitted that corrupt ambitions of men are executed under the guise of a divine benediction.

The old man sat bolt upright. "Are you accusing me?" The owl nodded as if in reply.

You do not require an answer from me. Are you prepared to unlock the truth in your heart?

Centuries of abuse, ignored through the illusion of sanctity, was starkly unveiled. Refusal to atone for mistakes or correct unacceptable behavior in the light of undeniable proof was painfully revealed. He writhed in agony at being forced to acknowledge the truth. "Oh, God! What have I done?"

Be comforted, my son. Not many men are prepared to truly search their hearts as you are doing. Self-deception is an enemy of truth.

He brushed tears from his eyes. "What is happening? Why are people turning from me?"

You cannot prevent it. It is impossible to hold fast to one rock as life evolves. Man cannot control all that he believes himself capable of mastering. Such determinations are the undoing of creativity and security. He is most creative and secure when his imagination is in harmony with the Universal Mind.

You became an immovable, institutionalized object, a construct of men attracted by position and authority. Well-meaning men who, nonetheless, failed to listen and respond to my voice within their hearts. They are unconscious of being lost in a wilderness of their own making. They became comfortable in their wilderness and eagerly draw others into the same desolation. There is no lack of people attracted by worthless glittering baubles or fleeting self-gratification. Human beings are basically lazy in mind and heart. Were they not, bleakness in the world would diminish rather than increase.

You long preached the wages of sin rather than the wisdom of balancing error with righteousness. People are hungry. They think they hunger for food and become obese on meals that do not satisfy their hunger. They are ignorant of what they truly hunger for. You ceased to feed your flocks with the food of life. When did you last praise people for having beautiful intuitive thoughts, lively questioning minds, recognition and appreciation of universal brotherhood? When did you last encourage them to pray from their hearts rather than mouth meaningless repetitions put there by you? When did you last pray from the honesty of your spiritual heart?

All eyes and ears focused on the venerable gentleman. The silent approach of black bears and elk was scarcely noticed. He thought long before replying. "Part of my role has been to draw people's attention to their sin and disobedience to your commands."

My commands?

"Your commandments to Moses, 'You shall have no other gods before Me. You shall not make for yourself an idol, or any likeness of what. . .'"

Enough!

"But I was only. . ."

Be silent. I do not command or impose laws. I created life to eternally perpetuate my love. As humankind evolved with increasing awareness of the essence of life, they began using my greatest gift to humankind – the power of reason. Decisions made from awareness of the essence of creation do not arise from commands, but from individual initiative through reason. Imposed laws to exercise control are meaningless; never born of a free will desire to be creatively self-perpetuating.

By now the forest floor was alive with curious animals, small and large. Never before had they heard the voice of God so clearly. Flying squirrels, nocturnal by nature, glided in from far and wide.

The man confidently stood upright and thrust out his chin. "You apparently have either forgotten or overlooked laws that abound throughout the universe. Without the law of gravity anything that was not securely anchored would fly from earth's surface; the moon would not be rotating around this planet; the heavens would be in disorder. Without mathematics no measurable structures could exist. Nature obeys laws of physics without exception. Moral laws are imprinted in all mortals from birth, perhaps from conception, but may be overlooked or set aside by creatively independent thinkers." He smiled, with a hint of smugness. "If not you, then who or what is responsible for the myriad laws governing this vast universe the human species is measuring?"

An excellent question. The answer is less complex than it might seem. I just said life was created to eternally perpetuate my love. The process required fundamental elements for creation to materialize. At the core of every atom in every element is a spark that exists for the purpose of replication. Self-replication required structures – patterns – known as laws. Without established structures – laws – there would have been chaos. Creation would have failed at its inception.

Here is an example. When you observe the smallest of insects with your naked eyes, you cannot be certain if that insect is aware it is being observed, or even aware of your presence. However, were you to threaten that insect it would immediately try to escape. That is one small example of self-preservation.

A more complex example is found in observing the processes of evolution. The concept of fight or flight includes development or decline. The ongoing process of life involves the formation of primary laws, or patterns, to sustain evolution. Intuition is the elemental spark of imagination. Imagination becomes the inspirational tool of creativity.

The fundamental force or law of laws, if you prefer, is creativity. Creative energy is born of and nourished through love. Love is an expression of appreciation for color, shape, movement, music, harmony and diversity in all forms of life. Life is a celebration of love. Do you understand the forces at work in my words?

"I am still pondering the significance of observing insects."

When you discover that you will understand the nature of reality and the illusion of belief.

An expression of utter confusion crossed his face. He grunted quietly from fatigue as his mind struggled to comprehend. But his mind was bound by centuries of traditional beliefs which became systemically self-perpetuating. At long last he replied, "Laws to which you refer must have been understood and accurately translated by elders in ancient times who received and recorded your words. Sages saw a decline in creativity in their communities. It was necessary to control lawlessness. Commands were required to subdue defiance of the law of creativity, as you say."

Commands remove people's responsibility to exercise reason in making important decisions. Your commands stripped them of initiative and independence. Self-serving commands increase rather than subdue defiance. You abandoned your role as leader to become a law enforcement agency. You refer to commands in your holy books supposedly issued by me. Would I command my children not to eat of the fruit of the tree of knowledge?

Did I not grow every tree that is pleasing to the sight and good for food – including the tree of life and the tree of the knowledge of good and evil – for a meaningful intent? Did I not create all things on earth to serve my purpose? Was I not pleased with my work? It is written that my sons feared humans would become as gods if they ate of the fruit of the tree of knowledge. Would a loving father want less for his children? Was it I who spoke those words?

Pause a moment. Allow your fertile mind to be still. Listen deeply, without interference from traditional understanding. Eating of the fruit of the tree of knowledge was the dawn of human self-awareness, self-consciousness, evolution of reason, the ability to recognize and classify external forms. The Garden of Eden became a symbol of mans' disgrace rather than his emergence from ignorance.

The man vigorously rubbed his brow. "Why are you confusing me like this?"

What need have I to confuse you?

"I don't know! My mind is in turmoil. If you are who you say you are, why do you not comfort me?" He collapsed heavily with his back against the tree.

A miniature winter wren boldly collected an insect that was caught in the folds of his garment.

I cannot deny myself. When will you allow me to be of comfort?

The man slowly lifted his weary head. Drooping corners of his mouth lifted into a smile. He breathed deeply, closed his eyes, then slowly exhaled. His frail body shivered slightly from release of tension. His face shone as he rose, stepped away and faced the tree. "I am beginning to understand."

Can you understand that it is essential for all intelligent beings to possess full knowledge of opposites in order to make choices for themselves? Another law that evolved through self-perpetuation is the law of cause and effect. Deny understanding of the consequence of wrong thinking and you remove an essential requirement for independent decision making. Individual personal responsibility is a vital constituent of life.

"We attempted to help people avoid making wrong decisions."

False! You attempted to control their minds and hearts, to dictate what was right and wrong. Some among you deplore people freeing themselves of tyranny. People see through your hypocrisy and turn their backs. You fear their independence because you are losing authority. People are becoming aware that truth resides in their inmost being. You believe repetitive words are sole revealers of truth.

My truth was placed inside souls for safe keeping against idolaters who prey as carnivores on minds and hearts. You failed to encourage awareness because it was lost to you. You were unwilling to recognize that fact. You complain that a secular conspiracy threatens the Church. Conspiracy? You dare to say that you have been the body of the Lord in the world and speak of conspiracy? Little man, who possess power to be my enemy? Who threatens the creator of the universe? Your churches are emptying because people have lost faith in many traditional beliefs. They have not lost faith or trust in God.

You may have enemies. Many claiming to be religious leaders have enemies. Fanatics see enemies everywhere. Ignorance abounds with enemies. By their bitter fruits are they known. Any man who dares to accuse others of being enemies of God has isolated himself from life. Wrong minded thinking turns a man against his inner Self. He alone removes himself and his misguided followers from life. Love of death supplants sanity. They remain ignorant of having lost their senses, yet believe they are defending what is holy.

The old man was visibly shrinking into his frail body. He struggled to speak. "I encourage my flocks to be perfect as the Lord Jesus said in his sermon on the mount. We believed we were being faithful to his teaching."

Your holy books are filled with wondrous teachings from my sons and daughters who heard my voice. By their good fruits are they known. Others made changes that were not in accord with truth, or misinterpreted what was originally spoken and heard. For example there is great misunderstanding about the meaning of perfection. I am not perfect in your understanding of the word.

The man gasped and looked up, eyes popping from his head. The forest seemed to catch its breath in astonishment.

You may well look surprised. It has long been taught that heaven is a place where no pain, no sorrow, no mischief and no misdeeds can enter in. Heaven is portrayed as a place of perfect peace and harmony and beauty – a desirable vision to ease the pain and sorrow from injustices that deeply penetrated the human psyche. Heaven is indeed a place of rest and renewal. But, understand this, the universe continues to evolve.

Your definition of perfection is anything that is complete beyond practical or theoretical improvement; without any of the flaws or shortcomings that might be present; faultless and correct in every detail. How can a universe be perfect when still in the process of developing? Do you not realize that life is not without flaws, not faultless and correct in every detail? Why then do you blame people for being imperfect? Why encumber them with the yoke of being born of original sin? That is a deeply erroneous burden to impose on innocent children.

My creation is perfect in the sense that it is ever changing, constantly evolving for the original purpose of perpetuating my love. Had I failed, life would not have continued to evolve for more than fifteen billion years of your time measurement. My love could not be contained. It literally exploded into life. You are an example of my love.

The man flushed with hope. "Me?"

Yes, you. We both made mistakes. You could not have known of my concerns whether creation would manifest as planned, or humanity would misuse freewill to exploit and corrupt gullible people and ignore the purpose of evolution. Once life began it was instantly free of control. I could not withdraw freewill when it was abused. Creative love cannot be controlled; otherwise it could not be eternal. It was life through my love that empowered forces to explode with energy that continues to radiate. Essences within that energy are the elemental substance of the universe. Self-centered love could not have sustained life.

Command and control? No. Life must be free of artificial controls if it is to be self-perpetuating and self-sustaining. It is the spirit of love within humanity, the problem solving mind that responds to prayer and performs miracles.

Religious leaders throughout the world have encouraged followers to worship me. I do not

*require worship. I do not need reminding who I am.
Humankind should be encouraged to grow in and
through me, to become as I am and continue the
process of creation through love. Because of men's
efforts to impose controls, rather than lead as
shining examples of love, they have all but forfeited
leadership. Hate grows stronger. If not reversed it
will destroy the world created by mankind.*

*Women could not be obedient to men who fell
into dishonor through selfish decisions and actions.
They were forced to assume leadership in many
areas where men displayed lack of wisdom. Sadly,
many women still suffer the effects of erroneous
decisions. Some are not yet free of the temptations
that corrupted their menfolk. Wisdom is a currency
of low value in the world. My children who came
into the world to remind others of the need for
divine wisdom were misunderstood. They suffered
at the hands of those they came to assist. You
cannot know the sorrow that spread throughout the
universe.*

The man looked up as drops of rain fell on his
head. He had not been aware of gathering clouds.
But the sky was clear. He then noticed water
droplets falling from tips of branches. No drops fell

22

from other trees. It then occurred to him what was happening. He rose to his feet, stretched his arms as far as he could around the giant tree and gently patted the soft bark in a comforting gesture.

"There, there," he murmured. "It is all right. I will do better. I will rid myself and the Church of carefully constructed dogmas and encourage your precious gifts to grow from the essence of your love, to flower and bear fruit for your eternally creative purpose."

Water ceased to fall from its branches. He continued to hug the tree for a long while. The forest was silent apart from a clear, flute-like whistle of a varied thrush. A surge of energy flowed into the man. Dropping his arms he stood back and reflected. The task before him was unimaginably difficult. It would be easier to move mountains than change hardened attitudes. Schisms within the Church were one thing, but gulfs between rational belief systems and irrational fanaticism are quite another matter. Traditionalists may dismiss him as a deranged heretic. Momentous inner change strengthened his resolve not to attempt to change the world, but to be true to his inner self and be a positive example to others. It might require another two millennia for true and lasting creative brotherhood to encircle the globe.

He smiled at the thought that it took evolution fifteen billion years to get this far. In the mind of God, he mused, humanity might just unite in brotherhood in less time. He turned and was delighted to notice the gathering of wild life.

"Thank you all for being my witness."

The inhabitants of the forest silently dispersed. He walked some distance then stopped, startled by the thought he might not again hear the voice of God. The same voice spoke quietly in his ear:

The decision is yours. When you truly confess that I can never desert you nor forsake you is when you will eternally be one with me. When you and all of humankind choose Life, you will then be released from inner strife. Do not worship me, simply be as I am.

"How?"

Do not force people to worship the god of your creation. My son Jesus was sent forth to bring my Light into a darkened world. Light is Love made manifest. Let the world know that without Love there can be no Light. Recognize and respect the

Light of diversity within yourself, in others, and the whole of creation. In so doing you will learn that nothing exists apart from my Love. Without Love – Light – eyesight would not exist. Recognition of that will enable all people to see with my eyes. They will see themselves more clearly, as I do, and will endeavor to reflect what they see rather than imposed or acquired distortions. Everyone who follows Jesus has his creative power, through Love, to do as he did, and more than he did. Guide all people to the Light of Christ and they will be as I am, through him.

He turned and gazed in wonder at the giant redwood tree that wept tears from God. He said with a broad smile and tears of joy in his eyes, "Thank you, Father."